Ainsworth Rand Spofford

The founding of Washington City

With some considerations on the origin of cities and location of national

capitals; an address read before the Maryland Historical Society, May

12th, 1879

Ainsworth Rand Spofford

The founding of Washington City
*With some considerations on the origin of cities and location of national capitals;
an address read before the Maryland Historical Society, May 12th, 1879*

ISBN/EAN: 9783337228927

Printed in Europe, USA, Canada, Australia, Japan

Cover: Foto ©ninafisch / pixelio.de

More available books at **www.hansebooks.com**

The Founding of Washington City

WITH SOME CONSIDERATIONS ON THE

ORIGIN OF CITIES

AND

Location of National Capitals.

An Address read before the Maryland Historical Society,

May 12th, 1879,

BY

AINSWORTH R. SPOFFORD.

Baltimore, 1881.

Fund-Publication, No. 17.

The Founding of Washington City

WITH SOME CONSIDERATIONS ON THE

ORIGIN OF CITIES

AND

Location of National Capitals.

An Address read before the Maryland Historical Society,

May 12th, 1879,

BY

AINSWORTH R. SPOFFORD.

Baltimore, 1881.

PEABODY PUBLICATION FUND.

COMMITTEE ON PUBLICATION.

1880–81.

HENRY STOCKBRIDGE,

JOHN W. M. LEE,

REV. E. A. DALRYMPLE, S. T. D.

PRINTED BY JOHN MURPHY & CO.

PRINTERS TO THE MARYLAND HISTORICAL SOCIETY,

BALTIMORE, 1881.

The Founding of Washington City.

THE founding of cities is to be ranked among the earliest of human institutions. Variously attributed to the gregarious instinct in men, to the necessity of protection and defence, to the ambition for creating a great capital, or to the natural accretions springing from the growth of commerce and the arts of life, the city has become a fixed fact in all civilized nations. What was the name or the locality of the first city is lost in the oblivion that entombs the populations, the language, and the literature of the pre-historic nations. We cannot even re-create the buried wonders of Persepolis, the capital of ancient Persia, nor can we tread with confidence amid the mythical splendors of Babylon. What were the features of that civilization which dwelt upon the banks of the Tigris and the Euphrates, may be conjectured for us by laborious antiquaries; but no authentic record gives us more than the scantiest memorials of their greatness, their wars, and their decline.

2   5

When we come to the cities of ancient Greece and Rome, we tread on firmer ground. In spite of the multitude of lost books, so greatly to be deplored, we have remaining precious and inestimable records, copious enough to reconstruct, with the added help found in the ruins of art and architecture, the cities of the past. The founders of the cities of Attica and of Italy, the *conditores urbium*, were reverenced, and often deified. The sentiment of religion (or of superstition, if you will,) presided over the genesis and the progress of every town. Surrounded by a sacred enclosure, and with a central altar on which burned forever the holy fire, the city was deemed the immediate and permanent abode of the gods of the nation. As pious Æneas brought the gods of Grecian Troy over many lands and seas to Latium, the city founded by Romulus was deemed sacred, and named Eternal. The tradition of the founding of Lavinium, whence the Romans sprang, has been preserved in the felicitous epic of Virgil, an intellectual creation which will long outlast the marbles of the Capitol or the Coliseum. Even now, the Romans celebrate the foundation of their city on the traditional day—the 21st of April.

So, in Athens, the reputed founders of the city, Cecrops and Theseus, were worshipped, and had temples erected to their memory. Tenedos, Delos,

Cyrene and Miletus, all worshipped their founders as tutelary deities, and Hiero, of Syracuse, who founded the town of Ætna, received divine honors after death. Indeed, the universality of this usage, both in Greece and Rome, is marked, and each city had its own peculiar and protecting gods, usually the heroes or ancestors of the people.

The wonderful ascendancy of the city of Rome in the ancient world was the fruit of her policy, much more than of her position. A city without seaport, seated on the banks of a river insignificant in size and incapable of extended navigation, she yet became so aggrandized as to win and retain for centuries the proud title of mistress of the world. It was not alone her military prowess, for the terror of her arms would have been powerless to hold subject provinces at vast distances, amid continual chances of revolt, and re-conquest. But the Romans pursued a policy which made Romans of their conquered subjects:—alone of all the ancient nations, they understood how to increase their population, and extend as well as consolidate their power, by war. They brought home enough of the inhabitants of conquered cities to make Romans of them, at the same time that they colonized the conquered countries with Roman citizens, institutions and laws. The wealth that flowed from the provinces made the rich city richer, and the aristocracy of Rome had the sagacity to admit to its ranks the wealthy citizens of the subject and allied cities.

Imperial Rome, like the Berserkers of Norse mythology, possessed the strength and the substance of all the cities which it subdued. It did more. It drew into its own overmastering pride of supremacy, the citizens of every conquered territory, sinking their nationality in its own. Municipal institutions died out both in the allied and the subject nations. The city was no longer seen anywhere except within the walls of Rome. She sent her citizens as governors or proconsuls into every land, to represent her sovereignty and to govern in her name. The Roman aristocracy became enormously enriched. The wealthy class alone filled the offices, which cost a great sum to purchase. A nobility was formed in the very midst of laws radically republican in form. Rich men alone composed the Senate, for it required a very large property to be a Senator. The grandeur of Rome was such that her ruling class, standing at the head of society in the most opulent city of the world, gave free course to their pride, luxury and ostentation. The Roman state itself, *civitas Romana*, was not enlarged by conquests; it kept with genuine conservatism within its ancient walls; what was increased was the dominion of Rome — *imperium Romanum*. This single city remained intact, while all the subject world it conquered—estimated at more than a hundred million souls—lost both institutions and laws, and became tributary to the centralized government at a distance.

The condition of the Roman subject was as deplorable, as that of the Roman citizen was enviable. The former had no rights, while the latter monopolized all rights and all privileges. Thence came the proud boast which made Roman citizenship a distinction unique in history. The people of other Latin cities were deprived of the suffrage, which was made the *peculium* of the Roman citizen. After a century or two of restless chafing under the rank injustice of this exclusion, the Social war followed, (B. C. 355,) which was waged by the Italian allies of Rome, that they might no longer be subjects, but citizens. It ended in the admission of the Italians to citizenship and suffrage. From that time all Italy formed one State, but the provinces had not been enfranchised. This came later, and by successive concessions of the Emperors, the Roman franchise was finally extended to all freemen within the Roman Empire. From that time until the destruction of the empire, all its territory, from Spain to the Euphrates, formed one people and a single State. The distinction between cities, kept up for centuries, disappeared.

The capital city, which at first contained only patricians as its citizens, thus gradually advanced in the extension of political privileges. First, men of plebeian origin were advanced to citizenship; then the Latins. next the Italians, and last of all, the provincials wherever found.[1]

It is a marked feature of the growth of great capitals, both in ancient and in modern times, that they almost uniformly seek the low lands, growing up upon the sea-shore or upon the banks of large navigable rivers. Of ancient cities most renowned for prosperity, wealth and population, there were located on the waters of the ocean or great tributary streams, Babylon, Nineveh, Tyre, Sidon, Carthage, Thebes, Memphis, Alexandria, Rhodes, Athens and Byzantium, now Constantinople. Later in the centuries, commercial supremacy was acquired by Venice, Genoa, Amsterdam, London, Paris, St. Petersburg, Liverpool, New York, Baltimore, Philadelphia, Boston, Chicago, St. Louis, and many other cities. all located immediately upon navigable waters. An Irish clergyman is said to have remarked, as a crowning proof of the beneficence of Providence, that it had caused all the finest rivers to flow past the largest towns. This putting of cause for effect is one of those ex-

---

1 The writer is indebted to the very able work of M. Fustel de Coulanges, "The Ancient City," for much of the material of the sketch of the Roman capital.

amples of inversion whimsical enough to be amusing.

The obvious advantages which a capital city reaps from a location upon tide-water are a double accessibility, cheaper means of transport and communication, and greatly enlarged facilities for commerce. It is generally believed that these advantages are purchased at some sacrifice of salubrity and of health; and we are pointed to the purer air of the highlands as more conducive to longevity, and to the more imposing and attractive scenery of mountain regions as better adapted to please the taste and elevate the mind. On this head it may be suggested that long experience shows men ever ready to risk health and comfort, and to sacrifice taste in the struggle to better their condition.

It happens by the ordinance of nature, that neither commerce nor manufactures can be widely or economically carried on without plentiful supplies of water—that element which covers more than three-fourths of the surface of the globe on which we live. By another ordinance of nature this element will not, unless under artificial compulsion, run up hill. It results that the two most profitable and most necessary avocations which aggregate men into cities—manufactures and commerce—avocations auxiliary to each other—the one furnishing the means and the other the market—

must ever be carried on in the lower instead of the loftier regions of the earth's surface. It would be unreasonable to expect a large population to plant themselves upon high ground, so long as food, clothing, and shelter continue to be the most imperious wants of man. It may be added that even the mountain worshippers are commonly content with paying their devotions at a distance from the elevated objects of their regard, a residence upon which, however sublime in theory, is very inconvenient in practice.

In point of fact, hardly half a dozen conspicuous cities of the world have been built on ground having much elevation above the sea. Jerusalem occupies heights 2,600 feet above the sea-level, but it was rather a seat of religion than of commerce, even in its palmy days, and it is now one of the most wretched and unprosperous places on the globe. Of all the capitals of Europe, there are but two having more than 600 feet elevation— Madrid, which is built at a height of 2,080 feet, in a region without industrial or commercial advantages, and Berne, capital of the little Republic of Switzerland, 1,856 feet above the ocean level.

In America, with the exception of Quito, the capital of Ecuador, 9,500 feet high, but so insignificant a town as not properly to come into comparison, Mexico is the only capital city which has any great elevation, 7,500 feet above the level of the sea. The causes which led the aborigines and their Spanish successors to build so extensive a city on ground so high would hardly have prevailed but for the fact that the Lake of Tezcuco and the heights of Chepultepee furnish an abundant and permanent supply of water. But the extensive remains of extinct cities at great elevations in some parts of the New World, would appear to indicate more exceptions to the general law in ancient than in modern times, and to lead to the conclusion that these buried cities were seldom or never commercial ones.

In the United States, we shall look in vain for any considerable city or capital built upon very high ground, unless we except such places as Salt Lake City, Denver, Colorado, and Virginia, Nevada, whose elevation of 4,000 to 6,000 feet is not local, but peculiar to the entire region in which they are situated.

Of all the State capitals, we find but one— Atlanta, Ga., having an elevation above 1,000 feet, and that has but 1,050, the greater part of which moreover, it shares with the surrounding country. Omaha comes next. which is 900 feet above sea level. while the elevation of St. Paul is 800 feet. From this we go down by gradations till we reach the sea level. Even some inland capitals like Hartford, Conn., can boast

3

an elevation of only 30 feet. Every one of the great maritime cities of the United States, New York, Philadelphia, Baltimore, Boston, Brooklyn and New Orleans, has an average elevation below 60 feet, Baltimore having the highest ground, Boston, 40 feet; New York and Philadelphia, 35 feet each, and New Orleans, only 10 feet. The largest inland cities, St. Louis, Chicago, Cincinnati, are only 475 to 575 feet above tide-water.

Passing from elevation of site to other characteristics, we shall find that large cities, and especially the capitals of nations, are almost invariably located rather with a single eye to convenience of access and commercial considerations, than with regard either to salubrity or centrality of position. In obedience to economic laws, we find the great capitals of Europe situated, several of them in unhealthy positions, as Berlin, Madrid, Rome, and Vienna, while the majority of them are placed without regard to the geographical centre of the country. St. Petersburg is in the extreme northwest of Russia, and the reasons for preferring it to Moscow, the former capital, were mainly commercial. Rome is on one side of Italy, though still more central as regards the north and south extent of the newly enlarged kingdom, than either of its former capitals, Turin or Florence. Constantinople hangs on the very southeast verge of Turkey; Lisbon, in the west of Portugal; London,

in the southeast of England; Copenhagen, in the
far east of Denmark; Brussels, in the north of
Belgium, while Paris is by no means near the
geographical centre of France, though doubtless
near its centre of population. Madrid, alone of
the European capitals, appears to have been con-
structed in the very centre of the kingdom, in
obedience to a purely geographical whim, without
regard to its position for commerce, which is remote from navigation, or its climate, which is
detestable.

It was remarked by Mr. Madison, in the first
Congress, that the States were tending more and
more to adopt central localities for their capitals.
Virginia had gone from Williamsburg to Rich-
mond, after the commencement of the Revolu-
tion ; North Carolina had adopted Charlotte,
and Pennsylvania was considering the plan since
effected, of exchanging Philadelphia for Harris-
burgh. New York has removed her capital from
the metropolis to Albany; Ohio has gone from
Chillicothe to Columbus; Michigan, from Detroit
to Lansing; Missouri, from St. Louis to Jefferson
city; West Virginia has adopted, prospectively,
Charleston in place of Wheeling. while Louisiana
will shortly abandon New Orleans for Baton
Rouge. These changes were in deference to the
sentiment which appears to weigh heavily in the
mind of the State legislator, that central geo-

graphical position is important for the seat of a State Government. The great majority of our States have located their capitals with approximate regard to this idea, the most considerable exceptions being Massachusetts, Florida, Kansas and Oregon.

The establishment of the National Capital of the United States involves so many particulars of historical interest, that no apology seems necessary for devoting to it the larger portion of this paper. In doing this, it will be my aim to touch with the greatest brevity on those portions of the history which have been fully brought out in the various publications on the subject, devoting the more attention to other incidents.

The Continental Congress, during the progress of the Revolutionary struggle, was never long fixed in any one location. Its sessions were convened at eight different places in four different States, viz: Philadelphia, Baltimore, Lancaster, York, Princeton, Annapolis, Trenton, and New York City.

After the final triumph of the cause of independence, Congress removed its sittings from Philadelphia, where they had been for nearly five years continuously held, to Princeton, N. J., on account of a turbulent interruption to their proceedings by a mob of mutinous soldiers, which the police authorities of Philadelphia had not promptly quelled. This untoward event led to much unfavorable comment, and exercised undoubted influence in determining against the location of the ultimate seat of Congress and the Government in any large city. The Congress of the Confederation was exercised by this subject at intervals, during the next four years, but as no vestige of its debates has been preserved, we can only judge of their course by the various resolves adopted.

The year following the removal from Philadelphia, December 23d, 1784, a resolution was passed to appoint three Commissioners to lay out a district from two to three miles square on the banks of either side of the Delaware, not more than eight miles above or below the Lower Falls, for a Federal town, a Federal House for Congress, and for the executive officers thereof, and houses for the President of Congress, the Secretaries of Foreign Affairs, War, the Marine, and the Treasury. This resolve, however, was not carried into effect. An attempt to amend it by substituting Georgetown, on the Potomac, was lost, Virginia only, voting in the affirmative, with seven States in the negative. The ultimate seat of Government thus received the vote of only one State in 1784.

May 10th, 1787, a few days before the meeting of the Federal Convention, Congress being then in session at New York, Mr. Lee, of Virginia, proposed to take up a resolution instructing the Board of Treasury to erect public buildings for the seat of Congress, at Georgetown, on the Potomac river, as soon as the State of Maryland should cede jurisdiction. This motion was lost by four affirmative to five negative votes; four States, Massachusetts, New York, Virginia and Georgia, voting for it, and New Jersey, Pennsylvania, Delaware, Maryland and North Carolina, against it.

The Convention for revising the Federal system of Government, assembled in Philadelphia, May 14th, 1787, (continuing in session till Sept. 17th, the same year.) On the 26th of July, Mr. Geo. Mason, of Virginia, proposed to provide in the Constitution against choosing for the seat of the General Government, any city or place where a State government might be fixed. He apprehended disputes concerning jurisdiction, as well as an intermixture of the two legislatures, tending to give a provincial tincture to the national deliberations. Mr. Gouverneur Morris, of Pennsylvania, feared that such a clause might make enemies of Philadelphia and New York, which had expectations of becoming the seat of the General Government. Mr. Elbridge Gerry, of Massachusetts, conceived it to be the general sense of America, that neither the seat of a State government nor any large commercial city, should be the seat of the General Government. Mr. Pierce Butler, of

South Carolina, was for fixing by the Constitution the place, and a central one, for the seat of the National Government. Mr. Mason did not mean to press his motion at this time, nor to excite any hostile passions against the system. He would withdraw it for the present. One week later, (August 6th,) in the report of the committee of detail to draft the Constitution, the provision as to a seat of Government for the United States had no place. But in the closing paragraph of the draft, as reported, Congress was empowered to "appoint a place for commencing proceedings under this Constitution." On the 11th of August, upon the clause as to power of adjournment in the two Houses, Mr. Rufus King, of Massachusetts, remarked that the section authorized the two Houses to adjourn to a new place. He thought this inconvenient. The mutability of place had dishonored the Federal Government, and would require as strong a cure as we could devise. He thought a law, at least, should be made necessary to a removal of the seat of Government.

Mr. Gouverneur Morris proposed the additional alteration by inserting the words, "during the session," &c.

Mr. Spaight. "This will fix the seat of Government at New York. The present Congress will convene them there in the first instance, and they will never be able to remove, especially if the President should be a northern man."

Mr. Gouverneur Morris: "Such a distrust is inconsistent with all government."

Mr. Madison supposed that a central place for the seat of Government was so just, and would be so much insisted on by the House of Representatives, that though a law should be made requisite for the purpose, it could and would be obtained. The necessity of a central residence of the government would be much greater under the new than the old government. The members of the new government would be more numerous. They would be taken more from the interior parts of the States; they would not, like members of the present Congress, come so often from the distant States by water. As the powers and objects of the new government would be far greater than heretofore, more private individuals would have business calling them to the seat of it; and it was more necessary that the government should be in that position from which it could contemplate with the most equal eye, and sympathize most equally with every part of the nation. These considerations, he supposed, would extort a removal, even if a law were made necessary. But in order to quiet suspicions both within and without doors, it might not be amiss to authorize the two Houses, by a concurrent vote, to adjourn at their first meeting to the most proper place. and to require thereafter the sanction of a law to their removal.

On August 18th, Mr. Madison moved to add to the enumerated powers of Congress:

"To exercise exclusively legislative authority at the seat of the General Government, and over a district around the same not exceeding —— square miles, the consent of the legislature of the State or States, comprising the same, being first obtained." This provision was afterwards moulded by the Committee on style into the form it now occupies in the Constitution, and adopted without debate. It is the last of the enumerated powers of Congress, except that to make all laws necessary and proper for carrying into execution the other powers:

"To exercise exclusive legislation, in all cases whatsoever, over such district, (not exceeding ten miles square,) as may by cession of particular States, and the acceptance of Congress, become the seat of government of the United States."

Very soon after the organization of the First Congress of the United States under the Constitution, the question of a permanent seat of government was brought up by a memorial from citizens of New Jersey and Pennsylvania, praying that the Capital might be established on the banks of the Delaware. But the First Congress

was very late in its own organization. The 4th
of March, 1789, prescribed by the Congress of
the Confederation in 1788, as the day for the
assembling of Congress, and the inauguration of
the new government, saw only thirteen out of
sixty-five Representatives ultimately appearing in
the First Congress present. Only five States out
of ten that had participated in the election of
President and Congress were represented at New
York. Not a member appeared from Maryland
before the 23d of March, nor from New York
(in whose capital city the Congress was held)
until the 8th of April, a week after the organization of the House had been completed. The
House secured a quorum on the 1st of April;
the Senate not until the 6th, and Washington,
who awaited at Mount Vernon the tardy official
notification from Congress of its readiness to
receive and install the new Executive, was not
inaugurated until April 30th, 1789, eight weeks
after March 4th.

It was not to be expected that the Representatives of what Washington called in his address
to Congress an "infant nation," so many members
of which were indifferent or doubtful as to the
success of a Federal Government, should have
been very zealous to unite upon a place for the
permanent seat of that government. New York,
by her municipal authorities, furnished to Con-

gress what were styled "elegant accommodations" free of rent. The claims of other cities and the offers of various States which soon began to pour in embarrassed the body. Trenton, Philadelphia, Germantown, Carlisle, Lancaster, York, Harrisburg, Reading, and Baltimore all were ready to receive the government with open arms. Maryland, by Act of her Legislature, December 23d, 1788, (six months before,) had authorized and required her Representatives at New York "to cede to the Congress and the United States any district not exceeding ten miles square which the Congress may fix upon and accept for the seat of government of the United States." Virginia passed a similar Act in 1789, referring to the advantages of a free navigation to the ocean through the Chesapeake Bay, and looking to the participation of the States of Pennsylvania, Maryland and Virginia in such location, on the banks of the Potomac. Congress divided into schools of opinion, difficult to reconcile. The subject first came up in the House of Representatives, August 27th, 1789, on motion of Mr. Scott, of Pennsylvania. "That a permanent residence ought to be fixed for the General Government of the United States, at some convenient place as near the centre of wealth, population and extent of territory, as may be consistent with convenience to the navigation of the Atlantic ocean, and have due regard to the particular situation of the Western country." Roger Sherman, of Connecticut, objected to the resolution. He wished to defer a question so important to the next session. The Union was not yet complete, North Carolina and Rhode Island being still to come in, and the continent ought to be properly balanced on this question. Besides, the government was not yet in possession of resources for the establishment of a Federal town.

Other members urged the importance of settling the question of the Capital as itself a new bond of union. Jealousies between the States could not be removed by postponing this question. Congress was now free from factions, and as devoid as possible of the spirit of party and local views. Hereafter, faction might lead to the choice of an improper place, from which they would have to remove after expending great sums, or the Union might be dissolved. On the other hand, members urged precisely the same considerations as arguments against deciding on a capital city. Fisher Ames counselled the House to move slowly, to get the government well organized before starting a question upon which the very existence and peace of the Union might depend. He doubted whether the government could stand the shock of such a measure, which involved as many passions as the human heart could display.

A motion to postpone the question to the next session was defeated—21 to 29. and it was made the order of the day for one week—September 3d. Before that day, the New England members concerted with those from New York and a part of the New Jersey and Pennsylvania delegations a plan to unite their votes for the Susquehanna river, as against any more Southern location. Mr. Goodhue, of Massachusetts, opened the matter by offering a resolution for "some convenient place on the east bank of the Susquehanna in Pennsylvania." Mr. Richard Bland Lee, of Virginia, offered a substitute providing for "a place as nearly central as a convenient communication with the Atlantic ocean and an easy access to the Western territory will permit." Mr. Daniel Carroll, of Maryland, seconded Mr. Lee's motion, which was vigorously opposed by New England and other members. Mr. Lee asked what objection could be brought to committing Congress in favor of a position central and convenient to the West. Would gentlemen say that the centre of the government should not be the centre of the Union, convenient to the ocean? The question to be settled was whether this government is to exist for ages, or be dispersed among contending winds. Mr. Lee's motion was defeated— yeas 17, nays 34.

Mr. Tucker, of South Carolina, thought any general resolution for a central position too vague. Is there any common centre? Territory has one centre, population another, and wealth a third. Was it intended to determine a centre from these three centres? The centre of territory might be ascertained, but that would lead to a situation entirely ineligible. He was for considering the several places to be proposed, according to their merits, without settling any principles by vote. The House, however, adopted Mr. Scott's motion by the decisive vote of 32 to 18. It was now apparent that the advocates of the Susquehanna were in control of the House. The Southern members protested against deciding the question without North Carolina, which would be entitled to six votes in the House. Mr. Jackson, of Georgia, was sorry that the people should learn that this matter was precipitated, and that the members from New England and New York had fixed on a seat of government for the United States. This was not proper language to go out to freemen. It would blow the coals of sedition and endanger the Union. He would ask if the other members of the Union were not also to be consulted? Were the eastern members to dictate the seat of government of the United States? Why not also fix the principles of government? Why not demand of us the power of legislation, and say,

give us up your privileges and we will govern
you? He denied the territorial centrality of the
place proposed. From New York to the province
of Maine, was only 250 miles. while from New
York to the nearest part of Georgia, was 1100
miles. Georgia would soon be as populous as
any State in the Union. If a decision was to be
made now, (which he deprecated in the absence
of North Carolina.) he hoped the Potomac would
be substituted for the Susquehanna.

Mr. Lawrence, of New York, said the eastern
members here were disinterested, since no plan
yet proposed contemplated fixing the seat of government in any of them. Had they consulted
their own interests, they would have chosen the
banks of the Delaware, but the Susquehanna was
nearer the centre of population in its present
period.

Mr. Sedgwick, of Mass., said the question had
been discussed as if there were impropriety in
the eastern members consulting on the subject.
It is the opinion of all the Eastern States that
the climate of the Potomac is not only unhealthy,
but destructive to northern constitutions. Vast
numbers of eastern adventurers have gone to the
Southern States, and all have found their graves
there.

Mr. Vining, of Delaware, said: "Though the
interest of the State I represent is involved in it,

I am yet to learn of the committee whether Congress are to tickle the trout on the stream of the Codorus, to build their sumptuous palaces on the banks of the Potomac, or to admire commerce with her expanded wings on the waters of the Delaware. I have, on this occasion, educated my mind to impartiality, and have endeavored to chastise its prejudices." This effusive gentleman proceeded: "I confess to the House and to the world, that viewing this subject with all its circumstances, I am in favor of the Potomac. I wish the seat of government to be fixed there, because I think the interest, the honor, and the greatness of this country require it. I look on it as the centre from which those streams are to flow that are to animate and invigorate the body politic. From thence, it appears to me, the rays of government will most naturally diverge to the extremities of the Union. I declare that I look on the western territory in an awful and striking point of view. To that region the unpolished sons of earth are flowing from all quarters. Men to whom the protection of the laws, and the controlling force of the government, are equally necessary; from this great consideration, I conclude that the banks of the Potomac are the proper station." The logic of this paragraph of the Delaware orator's speech is a little obscure.

Mr. Heister, of Pennsylvania, moved to insert Harrisburg, as more eligible than any place mentioned, having uninterrupted communication to the sources of the river Susquehanna, and capable of having water communication opened to Philadelphia at small expense. This motion was voted down.

Mr. Madison opposed the Susquehanna as not navigable, and it had been agreed on all hands that we ought to have some regard to the Atlantic navigation. As to the communication to the western territory, that by the Potomac was more certain and convenient than the other, while the water communication with the sea by the Potomac, was wholly unobstructed.

Mr. Clymer, of Pennsylvania, urged the superior navigable connections of the Susquehanna, which by the Juniata branch, and a short portage to the Kiskeminitas, opened a water way down the Alleghany to the Ohio river, at Pittsburgh. He questioned much if the navigation by the Potomac was so convenient.

Mr. Thomas Stone, of Maryland, said the people of that State were divided between the Susquehanna and the Potomac, both of which rivers watered its territory. While the majority might now prefer the Susquehanna, as their settlements extended westward and the population increased, the majority would be favored by the Potomac.

5

He would vote solely on national grounds, and if a central location was to be chosen, the importance of the Potomac could not be overlooked. Population was likely to increase in the direction of the milder, as distinguished from the severe climates, as men multiply in proportion to the means of support. If we looked to Kentucky, and compare its increase since the war with any part of the eastern States, we shall find men multiplied there beyond anything known in America. The agricultural States had not the same strong reasons for maintaining the Union as the commercial States; the western country might be inclined to drop off, and the Susquehanna was no bond by which to hold them, having its course northwardly rather than westerly like the Potomac.

Mr. Lee said it was well known with what difficulty the Constitution was adopted by the State of Virginia. If it should now be found that confederacies of States east of Pennsylvania were formed, to unite their councils for their particular interests, disregarding the Southern States, they would be alarmed, and the faith of all south of the Potomac would be shaken. Virginia had not solicited Congress to place the seat of government in her State, only contending that the interests of the southern and western country should be consulted: and he declared that these interests would be sacrificed if Congress fixed on any place but the Potomac.

Mr. Madison said that if the declarations and proceedings of this day had been brought into view in the Convention of Virginia which adopted the Federal Constitution, he firmly believed Virginia might not have been a part of the Union at this moment.

Mr. Sedgwick wished to know if it was contended that the majority shall not govern? Are we to be told that an important State would not have joined the Union had they known what would have been the proceedings in this House?

Mr. Madison replied that all which was asked was time for free deliberation. While he acknowledged that the majority ought to govern, they have no authority to debar the minority from the constitutional right of free debate. Facts should be gathered, and it was their right to bring all the arguments which they thought should influence the decision. To force a decision, as the majority seemed inclined to do, in a single day, was what he remonstrated against.

Mr. Ames said the House was ready to vote, and while he had no doubt of the patriotism and good intentions of the gentlemen from Virginia, they seemed to be engaged with a degree of eagerness which none else appeared to feel. They seem to think the banks of the Potomac a paradise, and that river an Euphrates.

Mr. Burke, of South Carolina, said the Northern States had had a fortnight to manage this matter, and would not now allow the Southern States a day. A league had been formed between the Northern States and Pennsylvania.

Mr. Fitzsimmons denied the assertion as it respected Pennsylvania.

Mr. Wadsworth, of Connecticut, said with respect to bargaining it would reflect no honor on either side of the House. He must either give his vote now, or submit to more bargaining. He did not dare to go to the Potomac: he feared that the whole of New England would consider the Union as destroyed.

The matter having been laid over one day, Mr. Madison again urged the importance of the most central position of the country as regards territory and population. Those nearest the seat of government would always possess advantages over those remote. An earlier knowledge of the laws, greater influence in enacting them, better opportunities for anticipating them, and a thousand other circumstances will give a superiority to those who are thus situated. If it were possible to promulgate our laws by some simultaneous operation, it would be of less consequence where the government might be placed; but if time is necessary for this purpose, we ought, as far as possible, to put every part of the community on a level.

Mr. Madison's sagacious observation here anticipated what we now see, all parts of a widely extended union of States brought to an instantaneous and equal knowledge of the doings of Congress by the lightning intelligence of the press.

He went on: "If the calculation be just, that we double in twenty-five years, we shall speedily behold an astonishing mass of people on the western waters."

Mr. Madison's calculation has been signally verified in the census of the United States, from 1790 (the year after he spoke) to 1870. In 1790, the population of the United States was four millions in round numbers; in 1810, seven millions; in 1830, thirteen millions; in 1850, twenty-three millions; in 1870, thirty-nine millions. This ratio of growth for each twenty years has more than doubled the population of the country each twenty-five years, with the single exception of the last quarter century, when it fell a trifle short, owing to civil war and decline of immigration.

On a candid view of the two rivers, said Mr. Madison, the seat which would most correspond with the public interest, was the Potomac. He defied any gentleman to cast his eye in the most cursory manner over a map, and say that the Potomac is not much nearer the centre than any part of the Susquehanna. The centre of population, he granted, was nearer the Susquehanna than the Potomac. But we were not choosing a seat of government for the present moment only. Population, said Mr. Madison, follows climate, soil, and the vacancy to be filled. The swarm does not come from the Southern, but from the northern and eastern hives. The Potomac is the grand highway of communication between the Atlantic and the western country. The gentleman from Massachusetts, who thought the Potomac subject to periodical maladies, should consider how much more liable to that objection were the waters of the Susquehanna.

Fisher Ames again urged the Susquehanna as nearest the centre, both of population and territory. Nearest the seaboard was the most convenient spot. With singular inconsistency, Mr. Ames argued further on against the Potomac, that it was exposed to danger by sea, since large vessels could go to Georgetown. West of the Ohio, was an almost immeasurable wilderness; it was perfectly romantic to calculate the increase of that part of the country; probably it would be nearly a century before its people would be considerable. As to the South, would gentlemen deny that trade and manufactures would accumu-

late people in the Eastern States in the proportion
of five to three compared with the southern? The
southern climate and negro slavery are acknowledged to be unfavorable to population. The seat
of government on the Susquehanna would be
nearly accessible by water to all the people on
the sea coast by the Delaware river on the one
side and Chesapeake bay on the other.

It will be seen how completely considerations
of transit by water rather than land, were made
the ruling ones in this debate. It also appears
how little actual knowledge had been acquired
of the depth or navigable quality of the streams,
when the lower Susquehanna was gravely talked
of as furnishing easy access to the ocean, and the
Kiskeminitas and Juniata were extolled as feasi-
ble water ways. On the other hand, the advocates
of the Potomac, who saw in the upper regions of
that rocky, shallow and tortuous river, a great
natural highway to the West, appear to have been
carried away by the undeniable beauties of the
locations presented by its banks, and its facile
navigation from tide-water at Georgetown to the
ocean, till they made nothing of the almost in-
superable barriers which nature has planted in
the path of making it a means of communication
to the Ohio.

Mr. Daniel Carroll, of Duddington, Maryland,
who lived on the banks of the Potomac, and who

was afterward one of President Washington's three Commissioners to lay out the District of Columbia, gave the Committee some facts respecting the navigation of the Potomac. A canal around the falls was now nearly finished, and soon an unimpeded passage would be allowed to the produce of the lands on its most remote and western branches. A debate ensued as to whether the cessions offered by the States of Pennsylvania, Delaware, Maryland and Virginia, of a seat of government, were intended to convey the soil as well as the jurisdiction. Mr. Carroll said that a cession of soil could not have been contemplated; because the State of Maryland had offered any part of the State, not excepting the town of Baltimore. If Congress were disposed to fix there, he believed it would be agreeable to the State; but he did not imagine they would agree to give the government a property to the whole town and surrounding country. The rest of the State never contemplated making to the inhabitants of Baltimore, a compensation for such an immense property.

Mr. Lee moved to strike out the east bank of the Susquehanna, in Pennsylvania, and substitute the north bank of the Potomac, in Maryland, which was defeated—ayes 21, nays 29.

Mr. Vining, having sacrificed a prejudice by giving a vote for the Potomac, would now bring before the House, the humble claim of Delaware.

He moved to insert the borough of Wilmington. This was lost by a still more decisive vote—19 to 32.

Mr. Boudinot moved to insert "the banks of the Delaware, not more than eight miles from the lower Falls." Lost—ayes 4, noes 46.

The question was then taken on a resolution authorizing the President to appoint three Commissioners to report the most eligible situation on the Susquehanna, in Pennsylvania, and agreed to, yeas 28, nays 21.

A proviso was adopted by a majority of one that the bill should not be carried into effect until the States of Pennsylvania and Maryland should pass acts providing for removing the obstructions in the Susquehanna.

The bill then (September 22d, 1789,) went to the Senate, where it was discussed three days, but as the Senate sat with closed doors, no records of the debates in that body were preserved prior to December, 1799. Here it was moved to strike out the words "in the State of Pennsylvania" from the bill, so that the place selected might be on the Maryland bank of the Susquehanna, if thought proper. This was lost—ayes 8, noes 10. A motion to substitute the Potomac for the Susquehanna was lost, vote not given. It was then moved to locate the permanent capital in a district of ten miles square at Germantown. Penn-

6

sylvania, on the Delaware, including such part of the Northern Liberties of Philadelphia as were not excepted by act of cession of that State. This was lost by a tie vote—9 to 9, but Vice-President Adams voting yea settled the question in the affirmative. In this vote the Northern and Eastern States were solid for Germantown, except Maclay, of Pennsylvania, who voted against it, while the Southern States were solid against it, except the two Senators from Delaware. A proviso was adopted requiring Pennsylvania to pay $100,000 toward the erection of the public buildings at Germantown, and the bill passed September 26th, yeas 10, nays 7. The same day the House had a discussion mainly unfavorable to the bill. Mr. Madison said that the place fixed (Germantown) had never yet been contemplated by the inhabitants of any one State, and that "the eye of America should be indulged with an opportunity of viewing it before it be made their fixed abode." Mr. White remarked upon the enormous price of land near Philadelphia, and the imprudence of fixing the seat of government there. On the motion to postpone the Senate's amendment to next session, the vote was ayes 25, noes 29. The next day, Roger Sherman argued in favor of the Germantown site as possessing some advantages over every other situation. Mr. Smith, of Maryland, opposed it. The price of land near

Philadelphia, was forty to fifty pounds an acre. Moreover, an objection against fixing near any large city was that the Federal town would in such case be no more than a suburb. The question being taken, the Senate's amendment was agreed to—ayes 31, nays 24, with a proviso continuing the laws of Pennsylvania in force within the ceded district until Congress should otherwise provide. The bill went back to the Senate for concurrence in this amendment, but it being within twenty-four hours of the close of the session, a motion to postpone the further consideration of the bill to the next session of Congress was carried. So narrowly did Pennsylvania escape having the Capital of the United States as a suburb to her chief city.

At the next meeting of Congress, January 4th, 1790, still at New York, several months elapsed before the question of the seat of government was reöpened.

Very engrossing business connected with the revenue, the funding of the public debt, &c., occupied the attention of both Houses. On the 31st of May, an attempt was made in the House to settle the question where the Congress should hold its next session. Philadelphia was proposed as the proper place, as a considerable majority had last session decided for Germantown as the seat of government. Mr. Smith, of Maryland, moved to meet in Baltimore, as more central. Its commerce was great, its inhabitants had raised a subscription of between 20,000 and 30,000 pounds to erect suitable accommodations for the members, and the Legislature had offered to cede to Congress ten miles square of territory. Messrs. Seney and Stone, of Maryland, and Mr. Lawrence, of New York, also advocated Baltimore. Mr. Gerry thought it unwise to remove from New York, where they enjoyed free accommodations. Congress could not remove with honor without reimbursing the city the expense. Mr. Thatcher, of Massachusetts, said business of the greatest consequence was before Congress, on which the public mind was very anxious, and it was no time to consider so trifling a question. It was not of two paper dollars consequence to the United States whether Congress sat at New York, at Philadelphia, or on the Potomac. The question being taken, New York was defeated, 25 to 35; Baltimore was lost, 22 to 38, and Philadelphia was carried, 38 to 22.

The question as to the permanent seat of government was renewed in the Senate, May 31st, 1790, by a bill offered by Mr. Butler, of South Carolina, fixing the place on the eastern bank of the Potomac. After reference to a select committee which reported it favorably, the Senate voted, June 8th, against the measure—yeas 9, nays 15. It was then moved to establish the capital at Baltimore, which was defeated by a vote of 7 against 17, both the Maryland Senators, Charles Carroll of Carrollton, and John Henry, of Easton, (afterward Governor,) voting against it, as did Delaware and Virginia, and all the Northern States, except a single vote from Connecticut. A motion to go to Wilmington was next defeated. The matter then slept for two weeks. On June 28th, the Senate again voted on Baltimore, which was lost—yeas 10, nays 15, both Senators from Maryland voting as before, in the negative. It was then moved to locate the permanent seat of government "on the river Potomac, at some place between the mouths of the Eastern branch and Conococheague." This was passed by the strong vote of 16 yeas to 9 nays, the Southern Senators voting solidly for it, with Maclay and Morris, of Pennsylvania; Elmer, of New Jersey, and Langdon, of New Hampshire. The President was authorized to accept grants of money to aid in the erection of the necessary buildings: and the sittings of Congress, with all the officers of the government were to be removed there in the year 1800. It was also voted, 14 to 12, that Congress and the officers of the government should be established at Philadelphia for the ten years commencing the first Monday in December, 1790. On the final passage of the bill, the vote stood 14 to 12, the site on the Potomac losing several votes from its first majority, for reasons not now known.

The bill was taken up in the House, July 6th, 1790, when it was moved by Roger Sherman, of Connecticut, and seconded by Mr. Burke, of South Carolina, to substitute Baltimore. Mr. White, of Virginia, said the Senate had repeatedly rejected Baltimore. Mr. Lee made a highly conciliatory speech, adverting to the necessity of cementing the Union, and maintaining the public credit. He alluded particularly to the great object of funding the debts of the United States; the seat of government will concentrate the public paper. The decision of the Senate affords a most favorable opportunity to manifest that magnanimity of soul which should embrace the best interest of the great whole. The States of Delaware, Pennsylvania, Maryland and Virginia, which contribute more than one-half to the revenue, and which have the only rival claim to the permanent seat of government, are satisfied with the arrangement in the bill. As to Baltimore, that was as far south as the place proposed, besides being exposed by its frontier position on the sea; he considered that motion therefore calculated to destroy the bill, and ought to be opposed by every one who was in favor of a southern situation.

Mr. Burke replied, exculpating those who favored Baltimore, from all design to defeat the present bill. One reason why he was in favor of the motion was, that he preferred Baltimore to Conococheague. He thought a populous city better than building a palace in the woods.

Mr. Lawrence, of New York, objected to the place on the Potomac as too remote. "The bill itself concedes that it is not at present a suitable position. Why was a period of ten years to expire? The reason is plain: the people would not now consent to have the government dragged to so remote a part of the United States. The public buildings could not be erected in the time mentioned. He then stated the advantages of Baltimore, and said that that place would have obtained in the Senate, if the Maryland Senators would have voted for it. He hoped as no necessity existed for removing the temporary residence, that Congress would sit down contented where they are. Mr. Smith, of Maryland, presented an address from the inhabitants of Baltimore, to the Representatives from that State, proffering every accommodation to Congress. Mr. Carroll, of Maryland, had read a memorial of the inhabitants of Georgetown, on the Potomac. Mr. Stone, of Maryland, had no election between the town of Baltimore and the Potomac; yet, as a Marylander, he would, if he saw a prospect of success, vote for Baltimore; but as it respected the United States, he should vote for the Potomac.

Mr. Seney, of Maryland, thought this an unhappy question to come before the House at this time. The State of Maryland is as much divided as the United States appeared to be; a great rivalship exists between the Potomac and Susquehanna rivers; and Pennsylvania and Maryland had formerly given the preference to the Susquehanna. He then noticed some transactions of the Legislature of Maryland, which he said clearly evinced their determination to support the pretensions of the Susquehanna.

Mr. Scott, of Pennsylvania, observed that from the town of Baltimore, there is no water conveyance to the interior country; but from the proposed site on the Potomac, there are two hundred miles navigation directly into the heart of the country. Nor is Baltimore more northerly than the position contemplated. A connexion with the western country is of the utmost consequence to the peace and union of the United States, let the gentlemen from the sea coast say what they will.

Mr. Madison would defy any gentleman, however sanguine he may be with respect to Baltimore, to point out any substantial advantage that is not common to the Potomac; "and I defy them to disprove that there are not several important advantages belonging to the Potomac, which do not appertain to Baltimore. In point of salubrity of air the Potomac is at least equally favored.

In regard to centrality of situation, the Potomac has undoubtedly the advantage. In respect to security from invasion, I aver the Potomac has the advantage also. With regard to the western country, there is not a shadow of comparison. If any argument could be brought against it, it was too far to the northward. The best evidence is the travelling of the members; the mileage south of the Potomac, is 12,782 miles; to the north of it, 12,422 miles. In my opinion, we should act wisely if we accept the bill as it now stands, and not consent to any alteration, lest it be wholly defeated and the prospect of obtaining a southern position vanish forever. He religiously believed that if Baltimore was inserted, the bill would never pass the Senate.

Mr. Gerry regretted that this measure of a permanent seat of government had ever been brought forward, for it was evident that it had a very pernicious influence on the great business of funding the public debt. He said it was highly unreasonable to fix the seat of government where nine States out of thirteen would be to the northward of the place. The explicit consent of the Eastern States ought to be obtained before they are dragged still further south. He ridiculed the idea of fixing the government at Conococheague.

Mr. Livingston, of New York, said the motion for striking out the Potomac and inserting Balti-

7

more, was so reasonable that he could not conceive there should be one person opposed to it. Baltimore was as far south as the Potomac. The members would have as far to go to one as the other. What advantage could it be to Congress that there was a river which runs two hundred miles into the country as far as the Alleghany Mountains? He could conceive none, except it may be to send the acts of Congress by water to the foot of the Alleghany Mountains. He enlarged upon the demerits of the Potomac, and asserted that taking so southern a situation would amount to a disqualification of many of the northern members, who would forego their election rather than attend the National Legislature on that river.

The question being taken to substitute Baltimore, it was lost—23 to 37. On motion to insert the Delaware in place of the Potomac, the yeas were 22, and the nays 39. On striking out and inserting Germantown—yeas 22, nays 39. On locating between the Potomac and Susquehanna—yeas 25, nays 36. On a second motion to insert Baltimore—yeas 26, nays 34; two Maryland members voting for it and four against it. The Senate bill for the Potomac was then passed without amendment—yeas 32, nays 29. An analysis of the vote shows that it was carried by the solid vote of the southern members, (except Seney and

Smith, of Maryland, and Tucker, of South Carolina, who voted nay,) united to the seven Pennsylvania votes, and one from New Jersey. The bill passed on the 9th of July, and received the signature of President Washington, July 16th, 1790.

North Carolina came into the Union with her five Congressional votes, just in time to take part in the settlement of a permanent seat of Government, and to decide the question in favor of the Potomac. We have seen that at the first session in 1789, there was a very decided majority against any site so southerly; that Germantown had afterward been agreed to by both Houses, though by very small majorities; that the Susquehanna had been carried as the site by a heavy majority in the House; that in the earlier stages of the second session in 1790, Congress was too closely absorbed with questions of revenue and public debt to consider the subject of the Capital city; and that finally, after long and sometimes acrimonious debate, a site on the Potomac was accepted by a majority of two votes in the Senate and three votes in the House. Those votes, moreover, could not have been obtained had North Carolina not come into the Union in the meanwhile, or had Pennsylvania sided with the northern vote as against the southern location.

Mr. Jefferson has recorded in his Ana, a remarkable piece of private history regarding the final adoption of the Potomac site for the National Capital. According to this statement, the session of 1790 was marked by an obstinate struggle over Hamilton's favorite scheme of the assumption of the State debts, amounting to twenty millions of dollars. This was at first defeated in the House; Hamilton was anxious and excited; he urged Jefferson to aid in securing its reconsideration, saying that the eastern or creditor States were dissatisfied, and threatened secession and dissolution if their claims were not considered. Says Mr. Jefferson:

"I proposed to him to dine with me the next day, and I would invite another friend or two, and bring them into conference together, and I thought it impossible that reasonable men, consulting together coolly, could fail by some mutual sacrifices of opinion, to form a compromise which was to save the Union. The discussion took place. It was finally agreed, that whatever importance had been attached to the rejection of this proposition, the preservation of the Union and of concord among the States, was more important, and that therefore it would be better that the vote of rejection should be rescinded, to effect which some members should change their votes. But it was observed that this pill would be peculiarly bitter to the Southern States, and that some concomitant measure should be adopted to sweeten it a little to them. There had before been propositions to fix the seat of government either at Philadelphia, or at Georgetown, on the Potomac; and it was thought by giving it to Philadelphia for ten years, and to Georgetown permanently afterwards, this might, as an anodyne, calm in some degree the ferment which might be excited by the other measure alone. So two of the Potomac members (White and Lee, but White with a revulsion of stomach almost convulsive,) agreed to change their votes, and Hamilton undertook to carry the other point. In doing this, the influence he had established over the eastern members, with the agency of Robert Morris with those of the Middle States, effected his side of the engagement; and so the Assumption was passed, and twenty millions of stock divided among favored States, and thrown in as a *pabulum* to the stock-jobbing herd."

So far Mr. Jefferson; and his statement has been generally accepted as a part of the history of the times.

It is a noteworthy fact that this act of Congress, adopted after so long and serious a division of opinion, fixed absolutely no definite place for the site of the capital city. It gave to the President of the United States the sole power to select any

site on the river Potomac between the mouth of
the Eastern Branch (or Anacostia) and the mouth
of the Conococheague; in other words, within a
distance of about one hundred and five miles
(following the river windings) from the present
site of Washington, to where the Conococheague
joins the Potomac at Williamsport, Washington
County, about seven miles from Hagerstown,
Maryland. Here was a wide latitude of choice
indeed, to be confided to one man. It was in
the power of Washington, under the provisions of
this act, to have founded the National Capital
at Harper's Ferry, fifty miles west of Baltimore,
instead of at a place forty miles south of it. He
might even have located it, at his discretion, at
the mouth of the Conococheague itself, one hundred miles farther up the river than the present
capital; and there is a contemporaneous letter
of Oliver Wolcott, which says: "In 1800, we are
to go to the Indian place with the long name on
the Potomac."

Washington, however, with that consummate
judgment which distinguished his career, fixed
upon just the one spot in the entire range of
the territory prescribed by Congress, which com-
manded the three-fold advantages of unfailing
tide-water navigation, convenient access from
Baltimore and the other great cities northward,
and superb natural sites alike for public build-

ings and for the varied wants of a populous city. The "magnificent distances" once the theme of so much cheap ridicule, are found not a whit too liberal, now that the capital has grown from a straggling village into a well-built and well-paved emporium for a population, which though not placing it in the first rank of cities, gives it at least an enviable place in the second rank.

Both Virginia and Maryland took the most active and zealous interest in the establishment of the National Capital on their borders. With co-terminous territory for nearly three hundred miles, separated by the great natural boundary of the Potomac, these prosperous commonwealths had every motive to unite in whatever should bring population and wealth to develop their great natural advantages, and to improve the navigation of the river. With a liberality equal to the occasion, Virginia voted $120,000 in money as a free gift to the United States Government to aid in erecting the public buildings, and Maryland appropriated $72,000 to the same object, a sum which was relatively a very large one in that day of small things. This not proving to be sufficient, and the Congress at Philadelphia not coming forward with appropriations, as had been expected, Washington was induced to make a personal appeal to the State of Maryland for a loan. He told Governor Stone that the Com-

missioners had attempted in vain to borrow in
Europe to carry on the public buildings, and he
knew of no place in the United States where
application could be made with greater propriety
than to the Legislature of Maryland, "a State
where the most anxious solicitude is presumed
to be felt for the growth and prosperity of that
city which is intended for the permanent seat
of government for America." The appropriation
was granted, and the Legislature accompanied
the act authorizing the loan of $100,000 with a
testimonial of their high regard for the President, while they were careful to require the personal security of the Commissioners (so low was
then the credit of the United States) in guarantee
of the repayment of the loan.

Washington appointed as Commmissioners for
surveying and laying out the Federal District
under the Act of Congress, Thomas Johnson and
Daniel Carroll of Maryland and Dr. David Stuart
of Virginia. Under his authority they marked
out the territory, which was so located as to
embrace the two towns of Alexandria in Virginia,
and Georgetown in Maryland, together with the
confluence of the Potomac and Anacostia, and
the commanding heights on both banks of the
two rivers. These Commissioners laid the cor-
ner stone of the new District, April 15th, 1791,
and under Washington's direction employed Major

Lenfant, a skilled engineer from Paris, to lay out
a plot of what they informed him in a letter dated
September 9th, 1791, they had decided to call "the
Territory of Columbia," and the Federal city, "the
City of Washington." The scheme of Lenfant
adopted as its basis the topography of Versailles,
the seat of the French government buildings, and
introduced those broad transverse avenues inter-
secting the streets of the city, with numerous open
squares, circles and triangular reservations, which
now form the main features of the plan of Washington. The proprietors of the lands within the
city limits relinquished all title in fee simple to the
President and Commissioners, conditioned upon
retaining for themselves an undivided half interest
with the Trustees in behalf of the public, in all
the lots laid off for sale; relinquishing without
compensation all lands occupied by streets and
avenues, and receiving twenty-five pounds an acre
for all which should be taken for public buildings or improvements.

The ideas of the founders of the city proposed a
seat of government of ample territorial propor-
tions, and provided for the future wants of a
teeming population. Thus, the public streets and
avenues were all from eighty feet to one hundred
and sixty feet in width, the latter being double
the width of Broadway in New York. There are
twenty-one avenues and thirteen parks or squares,

8

besides numerous smaller circles and triangular reservations, planted with trees. While the superficial measurement of the city proper includes 6,111 acres, not less than 3,095 acres of this surface is taken up by streets, avenues, and government reservations, leaving only one-half the surface of the city, 3,016 acres, to private houses and their grounds. There is thus a much larger proportion of land reserved from buildings in Washington, than in any other city in the country, a fact which secures permanent sanitary advantages of the utmost value.

This is no place for a description of a capital so often described. But it is a notable fact in connection with its history that the felicity of the site combined with the rival pretensions or disadvantages of other places, should have prevented a removal of the capital at seasons when that chronic discontent which sways the temper of many men and nations, broke out against the established seat of government. It is not strange that the early Congresses, amid the discomforts and deprivations which were inseparable from an infant settlement in the wilderness, should have wished that the spirit of compromise, or the influence of Washington, the father of his country, had been less potent in bringing the seat of Congress so far from the comforts and attractions of the cities they had known. These discontents

give an amusing and sometimes grotesque color-
ing to the correspondence and journals of the
early members of Congress and officers of the
government. Several abortive attempts to get
resolutions passed for a removal of the Capital
were made in the first decade of the century.
And in 1815, after the British army had destroyed
the Capitol, the Executive mansion, some of the
public offices and the Navy Yard, the spirit of
opposition to rebuilding at such a place as Washington became more pronounced. In point of
fact, not a solitary thing in the city (or rather
village) had ever been finished, and the crude
and comfortless situation of the public squares,
walks and streets, was paralleled in the half
finished condition of the public buildings. Some
were secretly glad that the British had burned
the Capitol, thus giving plausibility to the argument for rebuilding elsewhere, without sacrificing
the cost of what had been built. In February,
1815, occurred a long debate in Congress, very
imperfectly reported, on a bill authorizing the
borrowing of $500,000 at six per cent. for repair-
ing or rebuilding the Capitol, the President's
house, and the public offices on their present
sites. It was urged against the measure that
Washington as a Capital city was an entire fail-
ure; that the public buildings, if rebuilt here,
were subject to recapture or destruction by the

enemy at any time; that the interest and convenience of members of Congress and of the government required a place at or near some considerable city; that the centre of territory as well as of population demanded a location elsewhere; that this was no season, while the country was still in the midst of a costly war, to devote half a million to public buildings; and that even if it were deemed best to retain the Capital at Washington, it was absolutely needful to concentrate the public buildings toward the western part of the place, as near as possible to Georgetown, rather than rebuild them on the existing distant and highly inconvenient sites.

On the other hand it was urged with great force that to talk of removing the Capital then, was untimely and pusillanimous; that Congress would never recover from the odium of having run away in the face of the enemy, taking their Capital with them; that the site of the Federal city had been determined on after full deliberation by the founders of the Republic, and under the immediate care of Washington; that it combined great natural advantages with remoteness from the disturbing influences of a populous city; that to suffer a single day's invasion and vandalism of an enemy, at the National Capital, to break up the seat of Government of the United States, would be too pitiful a spectacle to present to the eyes of the world; that to rebuild the public edifices on the old sites would save at least one-half the expense, because the old walls could be largely used; that to remove the Capital would be grossly unjust to the people of the District, some of whom had given their lands, and others had invested their property here on the faith of the permanent residence of the government, and they would now have just claims to indemnification to a heavy amount; that it would be equally unfair to Maryland and Virginia, which States had given nearly $200,000 to help erect the government buildings; that the continual agitation of the question of removal, of retrocession, etc., was the sole cause why the city of Washington had not grown in proportion to the other places on the continent; and that no prudent man could be expected to risk his fortune in a place that was every year threatened with destruction by the very power which ought to foster and protect it.

The result of this full discussion was the triumph of the conservative influence which favored the retention of the Capital at Washington. The bill appropriating $500,000 was carried by a majority of fifteen in the House, and by a small vote in the Senate; and though the struggle was more than once renewed on occasion of after demands for building purposes, the Capital movers won no victory.

When the project for ceding back to Virginia, the town of Alexandria, and the lands of the District lying west of the Potomac, was brought forward in 1846, the matter of removal was again discussed. The motives of the people of Alexandria for desiring to be relegated to a union with Virginia were obvious enough. In the half century of their attachment to the District of Columbia, the sanguine hopes which a former generation had built upon the fostering hand of the National Government had not been realized. Congress had done little or nothing for the improvement of that side of the river. Washington had grown from a little settlement of 500 souls to a population of nearly 40,000; but Alexandria had not shared this rapid increase, and found her commerce, instead of the vast extension which had been predicted, growing even smaller year by year. Her people, deprived of the privileges of citizenship in Virginia, had acquired no rights under the United States: on the contrary, they were deprived even of the privilege of voting for President or Congress, while at the same time without a voice in any of the laws that governed them. In the forcible language of one of their spokesmen, they were "political orphans, who had been abandoned by their legitimate parents, and were uncared for by the parents who had adopted them." Mr. Reverdy Johnson said that the people of Alexandria complained of having been neglected by Congress, and they had probably good reason, since it was natural that Congress should be more favorable to that part of the District which was the immediate scene of its labors.

Mr. Calhoun, replying to the constitutional objection to retrocession, that it proposed to cede a part of the permanent seat of the government, said the Act of Congress so providing possessed no perpetuity of obligation, but was repealable. Besides, the giving up of a strip of land on the other side of the river could in no manner affect the permanency of the seat of government in what remained. Here the government had been wisely located, and here in his opinion it would continue, so long as the institutions of the Republic endured.

Mr. William Allen, of Ohio, said he was for establishing the seat of government to the westward, near the centre of the country. Its location near the seaboard and the chief commercial cities gave to the commercial interest a preponderating influence over legislation. There were no lobbies from the farmers of the west, but the committees of Congress were overrun with tariff lobbyists and Wall street lobbyists. The great mass of the people—four-fifths of them—lived on the soil, and it was in their centre that the seat of government should be located.

Mr. Calhoun replied that at the Memphis Commercial Convention, a body composed of six hundred members, representing almost exclusively the interests of those who lived on the soil, a resolution was offered recommending a change in the seat of the General Government. A most extraordinary sensation was produced, and when the resolution was submitted, there was one loud-toned, overwhelming No! opposed to the solitary voice of the mover.

The retrocession was carried by a large majority in both branches of Congress. It submitted the question to a vote of the people concerned, and the reunion with Virginia was ratified by a vote closely approximating unanimity.

Of the chances and changes which have come to Washington during and since the civil war period; of the career of its short-lived, but preternaturally active territorial government and Board of Public Works; of the sudden transformation of the city since 1871, with a vigor and completeness almost without parallel in municipal annals, from a rude, unpaved, marshy, uncomfortable and repulsive town, to a city of magnificently improved smooth streets and avenues; of the great debt piled up in the process, with the incidental costly blunders, extravagance and waste; of the final adjustment by Congress of the share which the general government is to bear in the future care and improvement of the city, at one-half of the total expenditure; in short, of that marvellous renovation which has made Washington a new city, almost unrecognizable by those who have not seen it since the days before the war—this is no place to speak. Suffice it to say, that this seat of the political union of a great nation, founded by the illustrious Washington whose name it bears, "the only child of the Union," —as Senator Southard styled it forty years ago—has reached a point where it presents itself as fully worthy of its parentage. With its un-surpassed natural advantages, its sightly and beautiful location, its genial climate, its suburban scenery and attractions, its magnificent public buildings, its fine broad avenues and pleasantly shaded streets, its free gallery of art, its noble libraries and extensive museum of science, its national observatory whose telescope has added new stars and satellites to the sky, its men of learning devoted to every field of research, and its rapidly growing wealth and population, Washington has outlasted the possibility of decadence.

As the seat of so many notable events in our political history, the forum of debate where the great questions of constitutional law and national welfare have been decided, the place of the graves of many illustrious dead, the repository of the records of a government which, though scarcely a century old, is rich in national archives, the Capital presents a perennial attraction to American citizens. While overshadowed by Baltimore and other cities in commerce, manufactures, shipping and population, it has yet enough of interest without these advantages. The time will soon come, if it has not already arrived, when the most infatuated of Capital movers will look upon the task of tearing down Washington with dismay. Of the nine millions of American pilgrims who visited the great World's Fair and Centennial Celebration, at Philadelphia, in 1876, a very large proportion made the pilgrimage to Washington. As they walked through the noble marble corridors of the Capitol, and from the dome or the porticos gazed across the broad Potomac, or followed the outlines of the great city spreading wide up to the very edges of its amphitheatre of hills, a genuine feeling of pride animated almost every heart. They returned to their homes, elevated with the experience, with a new and more fervent sentiment of loyalty to our common country, and breathing for the great Republic a prayer that it may last forever.